A Visit to CHINA

By Charis Mather

Minneapolis, Minnesota

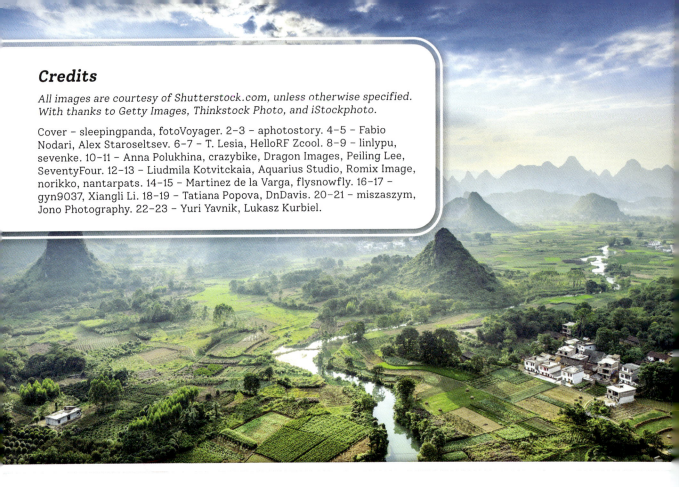

Credits

All images are courtesy of Shutterstock.com, unless otherwise specified. With thanks to Getty Images, Thinkstock Photo, and iStockphoto.

Cover – sleepingpanda, fotoVoyager. 2–3 – aphotostory. 4–5 – Fabio Nodari, Alex Staroseltsev. 6–7 – T. Lesia, HelloRF Zcool. 8–9 – linlypu, sevenke. 10–11 – Anna Polukhina, crazybike, Dragon Images, Peiling Lee, SeventyFour. 12–13 – Liudmila Kotvitckaia, Aquarius Studio, Romix Image, noriko, nantarpats. 14–15 – Martinez de la Varga, flysnowfly. 16–17 – gyn9037, Xiangli Li. 18–19 – Tatiana Popova, DnDavis. 20–21 – miszaszym, Jono Photography. 22–23 – Yuri Yavnik, Lukasz Kurbiel.

Library of Congress Cataloging-in-Publication Data is available at www.loc.gov or upon request from the publisher.

ISBN: 979-8-88509-038-4 (hardcover)
ISBN: 979-8-88509-049-0 (paperback)
ISBN: 979-8-88509-060-5 (ebook)

© 2023 Booklife Publishing
This edition is published by arrangement with Booklife Publishing.

North American adaptations © 2023 Bearport Publishing Company. All rights reserved. No part of this publication may be reproduced in whole or in part, stored in any retrieval system, or transmitted in any form or by any means, electronic, mechanical, photocopying, recording, or otherwise, without written permission from the publisher.

For more information, write to Bearport Publishing, 5357 Penn Avenue South, Minneapolis, MN 55419. Printed in the United States of America.

CONTENTS

Country to Country 4
Today's Trip Is to China! 6
Beijing 8
Chinese New Year 10
Food 12
Panda Bears 14
Rivers 16
Terracotta Army 18
Amazing Buildings 20
Before You Go 22
Glossary 24
Index 24

COUNTRY TO COUNTRY

Which country do you live in?

A country is an area of land marked by **borders**. The people in each country have their own rules and ways of living. They may speak different languages.

Each country around the world has its own interesting things to see and do. Let's take a trip to visit a country and learn more!

Have you ever visited another country?

TODAY'S TRIP IS TO CHINA!

China is a country in the **continent** of Asia.

FACT FILE

Capital city: Beijing
Main language: Mandarin Chinese
Currency: Renminbi
Flag:

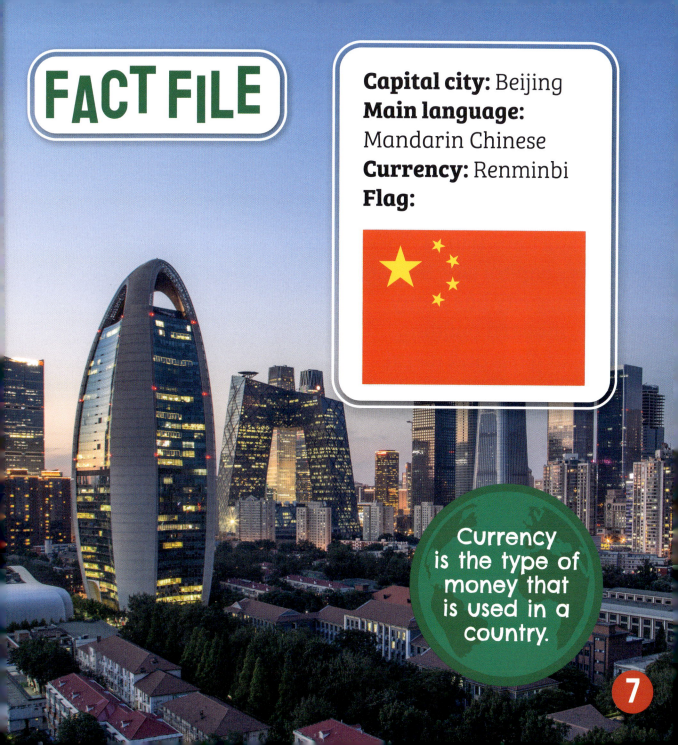

Currency is the type of money that is used in a country.

BEIJING

We'll start our trip in China's capital city, Beijing. This busy city has many large, **modern** buildings made of glass and metal.

Some of Beijing's buildings are home to millions of people.

Beijing is also known for its long history. The city has historical buildings called *siheyuan*, which are very different from the modern buildings. A *siheyuan* has four sides around an open area.

CHINESE NEW YEAR

Next, let's **celebrate** a holiday! Chinese New Year is China's biggest celebration. Families get ready by cleaning their homes and decorating. Many people go out to watch fireworks.

People may celebrate with a **traditional** dragon dance. Many dancers work together with a big dragon puppet.

Most families celebrate by sharing a large meal. There are lots of dishes, including dumplings, sticky rice cakes, and fish. Older family members give children red envelopes full of money as gifts.

Red is a lucky color in China.

FOOD

Different parts of China have different types of food. Some people eat noodle dishes as their main food, and some eat rice dishes. Chinese food can be salty, sweet, spicy, sour, or a mix.

Chinese dishes are often eaten with chopsticks.

Here are some popular Chinese foods!

Dumplings are filled with meat and vegetables.

Some people have noodles for breakfast.

Hot pot is a meal to share. Everyone adds their favorite food into a soup.

PANDA BEARS

Next, let's visit some panda bears! Pandas are among China's most-loved animals. Some pandas live in mountain forests where they can find lots of bamboo to eat. They spend about 14 hours a day eating bamboo.

Other pandas live in **nature reserves**. People there look after the pandas and their cubs. When the baby pandas have grown up, some are sent to live in the wild.

This panda cub is only three months old.

RIVERS

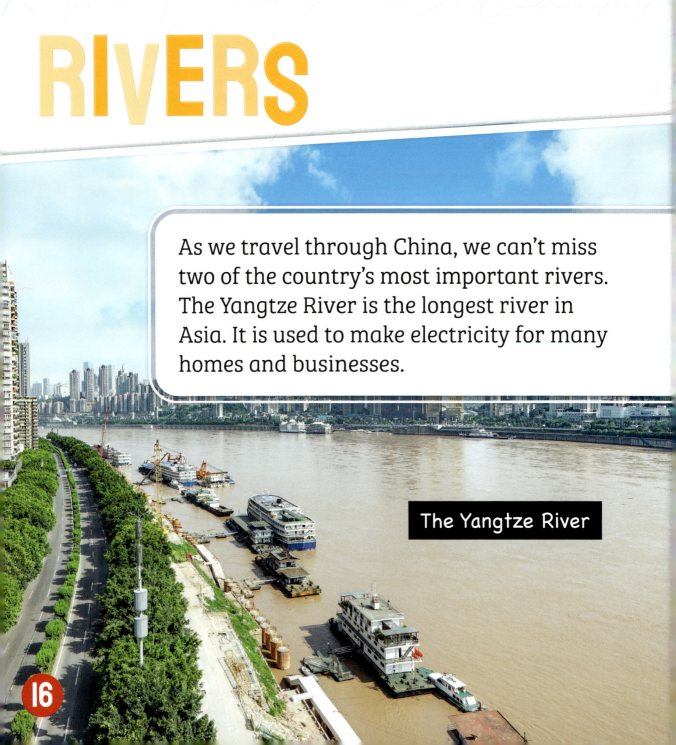

As we travel through China, we can't miss two of the country's most important rivers. The Yangtze River is the longest river in Asia. It is used to make electricity for many homes and businesses.

The Yangtze River

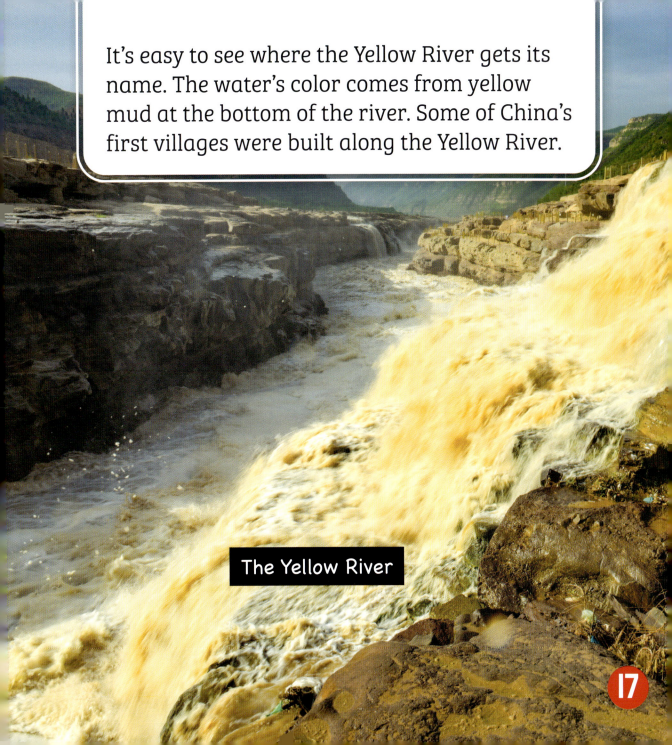

It's easy to see where the Yellow River gets its name. The water's color comes from yellow mud at the bottom of the river. Some of China's first villages were built along the Yellow River.

The Yellow River

Terracotta Army

The Terracotta Army has clay **soldiers** and horses.

A big historical site lies underground near the city of Xi'an. Thousands of clay statues were uncovered in 1974. The statues are called the Terracotta Army.

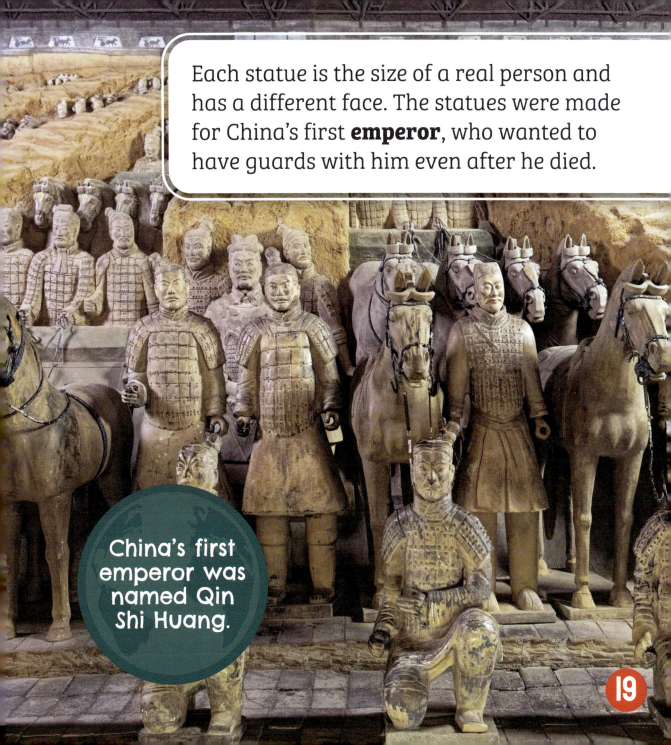

Each statue is the size of a real person and has a different face. The statues were made for China's first **emperor**, who wanted to have guards with him even after he died.

China's first emperor was named Qin Shi Huang.

AMAZING BUILDINGS

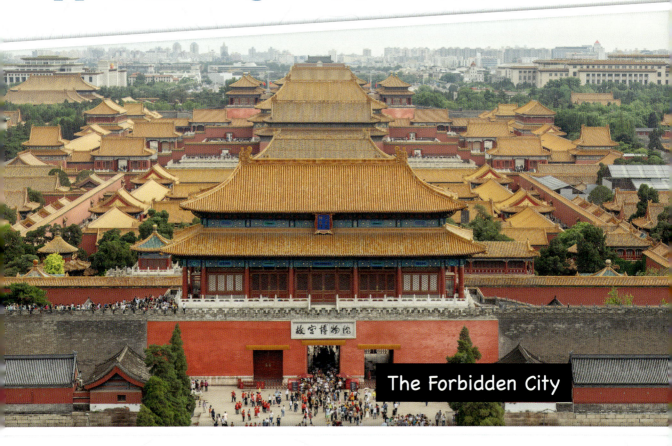

The Forbidden City

The Forbidden City in Beijing is also an important part of China's history. Many emperors lived there with their families. The Forbidden City has thousands of rooms.

We can also stop by the Hanging **Monastery**. It is much smaller than the Forbidden City, but it's still impressive. The building hangs from the side of a mountain. The monastery was used by people from three different Chinese religions.

The Hanging Monastery

BEFORE YOU GO

The Great Wall of China

We can't forget to see the Great Wall of China! The wall was built by many people over thousands of years. It is more than 13,000 miles (21,000 km) long.

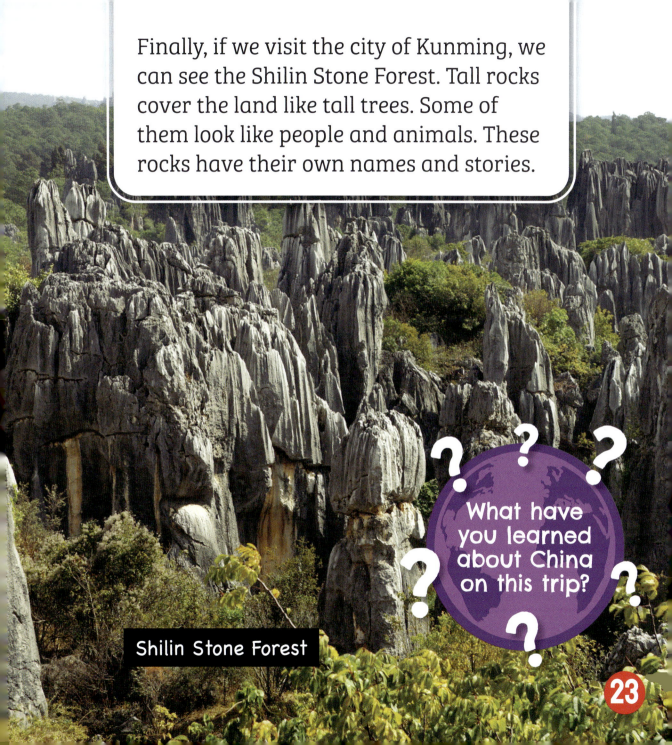

Finally, if we visit the city of Kunming, we can see the Shilin Stone Forest. Tall rocks cover the land like tall trees. Some of them look like people and animals. These rocks have their own names and stories.

Shilin Stone Forest

What have you learned about China on this trip?

GLOSSARY

borders lines that show where one place ends and another begins

celebrate to come together and enjoy a special event

continent one of the world's seven large land masses

emperor the ruler of a large area of land called an empire

modern new and different from the past

monastery a religious building

nature reserves areas of land where people keep plants and animals protected

soldiers people trained to fight in battles

traditional relating to something that a group of people has done for many years

INDEX

buildings 8–9, 20–21
celebrations 10–11
dragons 10
emperors 19–20, 22
forests 14, 23
history 9, 17–18, 20
mountains 14, 21
rice 11–12
statues 18–19